TO

_____

FROM

_____

Please see the end of this book for more dedications.

iii

ISBN (eBook): 978-0991265312

Print Edition ISBN: 978-0991265329

Photos are courtesy of the writer and

www.wallpaperswala.com

Published by

www.athospress.com

Fathers & Daughters

A Fatherhood Legacy

2nd Edition

George G. Spanos

Athos Press

George G. Spanos is 41 years old.

He is a father of three daughters and a stepfather of three sons. This is the 2nd edition of his first book on Fatherhood Legacy series, soon to be followed by "Stepfathers & Sons".

His other books in print are adaptive translations in Greek and in English of popular books by C.S. Lewis, Anthony Flew, and other contemporary spiritual and non-fiction writers that are related in any way with Mount Athos.

His on-going studies include Philosophy & Humanities in Athens, Mech. Engineering & Shipping in London, Hellenic Studies & Early Christianity in Harvard.

Apart from being an active entrepreneur in Shipping he has received honors and distinctions for his services as a Diplomat and for his participation in several charity and cultural boards in Greece.

For more info visit

www.amazon.com/author/georgespanos

www.facebook.com/george.g.spanos

www.about.me/george.g.spanos

To

Marina, Maria, & Anastasia

who inspired my life,

before

they were born.

Contents

Prologue

This book is not written by a professional writer or a theoretical professor in pedagogical studies. It is written by someone who actually is a father of daughters and knows exactly what he is talking about when he describes this unique relationship. A father who's been happy, proud, sad, anxious, frustrated; who's cried from joy and sorrow for his daughters. Who's *put his finger into the print of the nails* of fatherhood and (still) enjoys the everyday experience and challenge of raising girls into successful women in terms, mainly, of character and personality, with which they will try to make a difference through the roles they'll choose to follow in their lives.

There are indeed a few books about fathers and daughters around. I would humbly say that this one is a supplement to and not a substitute for the others, a book that gives different, basic, and condensed messages about those things a father and a daughter need to realize about each other and be reminded of, occasionally.

Through his parenthood function, today a father has to stay focused on passing strong quality values to his daughter(s) and not be swept away by the multiplex influences that prevail but are ephemeral and empty.

This book is written for all fathers and daughters of this world without exception, including those who are also mothers, simply because it provides them with a stimulating food for thought on how to support the irreplaceable role of father figure to their children.

I believe that since a father, even the best one, cannot always (and one day will not) be physically there, this book can serve as a representative spiritual testament of his legacy.

In this paperback edition, the reader, father or daughter, is strongly urged to inscribe a personal dedication at the front and contribute to this endless bequest by adding his or her own notes in the very end of the book.

G. S.

Fathers & Daughters

A father and a daughter

need each other's hugs and kisses,

from the day she comes into this world

until the day he departs from it.

A daughter likes

that her father is one of the few

people in the world that knows

so many things.

Among

men and women,

genuine friendship,

wholesome affection,

and unconditional love

can only exist altogether

between fathers and daughters.

The only occasion

when a man really faces

"the most beautiful woman in the world"

is when a father gazes on his sleeping

daughter.

The most appropriate person

to teach a future woman why

she deserves to be treated well by men

is her father.

A loving dad can convince his daughter

that the most important and critical role of her

life, no matter what the world thinks,

will be the role of a wife and mother.

. . .

And don't let her forget that

what the world thinks

about anything is never really important.

Only a faithful father can teach his daughter

that when her heart and consciousness

are filled with peace and not with

anxiety or fear, it is then that

she experiences Grace.

And that pure boldness

derives mainly from a clear

conscience and undoubting faith

in God.

The best way a dad can merge bravery and

heroism with his daughter's femininity,

is by drawing her attention to everyday women

that proved they didn't belong to the

weaker sex.

A daughter must learn from her dad

how to recognize and practice the virtues

she inherited from him, and her father should

unashamedly help her learn from the mistakes

he has made in his life.

A father can estimate

how well he raised his daughter

by observing how she behaves

toward her own children

and whether she chooses

to present him as an

example to them.

A daughter who missed out on the love

and affection of her father will be

the woman who will try to get

both of them from the first man

who will show the slightest

interest in her.

. . .

Unfortunately,

most women who feel

worthless and without hope

were never as little girls

encouraged by their fathers.

Our daughters need us to fight for them.

Otherwise they will look for someone who will.

And chances are he won't be

the right one.

Daughters

who received love and care

from their fathers can easily sense

the meaning (and the presence)

of healthy and successful

relationships throughout

their lives.

A father who is for any reason divorced

must constantly and primarily

remind and prove to

his daughter that

he will never

for any reason

be detached from her and

that he will help her avoid the

mistakes that he and her mother made, so

she won't hesitate to make a family of her own.

The best legacy

a father can leave to his daughter

is his enthusiasm for being her father and the

happiness he has derived

from it.

. . .

When a father

says "I love you" to his daughter

he never says it by rote.

There's nothing

a father wouldn't do to earn his

daughter's trust.

. . .

The road

is never too long

for a father visiting his daughter.

One of the greatest successes

a father can have with his daughter

is to help her adopt consciously those

two endangered characteristics

that are indistinguishable

in today's deceitful

world:

respectful sincerity

and

sensible honesty.

The best vote of confidence a daughter

can give her father is standing

beside him if he chooses to

remarry.

Only a Father . . .

...is able to pass on to his daughter how bad it

will be for herself and her husband

if she can't control the bad habit

of niggling and bed nagging...

...even though, as a dad, he always

enjoyed her chatter when he was trying

to put her to sleep.

Only a father

can remind to his daughter that

a little jealousy between

a couple

is beneficial,

whereas too much totally

destroys their relationship.

Only a father

Can teach his daughter early on

that the most precious and irreplaceable

thing in her life is Time and that's why

she must learn to manage it wisely.

Only a father

who has realize

how ironic is the concept of possession,

can let her daughter know that the

only things she will ever get to really own,

and will accompany her life for ever,

are those she will give to and share with others.

Only a father

can illustrate to his daughter that

ungratefulness is a relentless poison

that kills a relationship,

still in small doses

. . .

Even Jesus Christ Himself was not

only shocked (remember the lepers?)

but was ultimately crucified due to it.

Only a father

Can ascertain his daughter that in her life

she must be always prepared to deal

with the mean and the ungrateful,

especially those whose she's helped.

At the other hand, he has to remind her

not to be unthankful herself,

when her husband will fail

to satisfy one of her 100 favors

by writing-off the other 99

he has satisfied.

Only a father

can refrain his daughter

from disregarding her dedicated

husband or friends,

because when dedicative people feel ignored,

or taken for granted,

they can always take the chance

to cross the open door

and dedicate

themselves elsewhere.

Only a father

can teach his daughter

that forgiveness and repentance

is not an act of weakness

but of the utmost strength.

can convey to his daughter that a real man

will always sacrifice himself for her,

as long as she doesn't take him

for granted. . . .

. . . even though her father allowed himself

to be putty in her hands, she must never treat

her husband in the same manner.

Only a father

can prepare his daughter against those men

who seem to know how to speak to women

by telling them all the things they

might want to hear, and

to remind her not to give her attention to any

man who desperately seek it.

It Takes a Daughter . . .

...to make a father realize

how boys should be raised, too;

so they can become successful men

and fathers themselves.

. . .

...not only to turn a father into a hero,

but to give him the aspiration to raise a heroine.

. . .

...to remind a father

that he must always stay sensible and honest,

even when he doesn't want to.

It takes a daughter

to teach a father that the force with which

a man should impose himself on a woman

is not his voice or his hand,

but the sacrifice that

derives from his

love for her.

. . .

And to remind a father that

genuine respect is earned and not coerced.

It takes a daughter

to inspire a father never to

give up after a failure

but to confront difficulties

by turning them into benefits;

and show her how someone mustn't remain

"under the circumstances"

but override them.

A Father Will Always . . .

. . .be his daughter's first inspiration,

the one who will lead her close to or away

from God.

A father will always

turn back time in his mind

and see his daughter in his t-shirt,

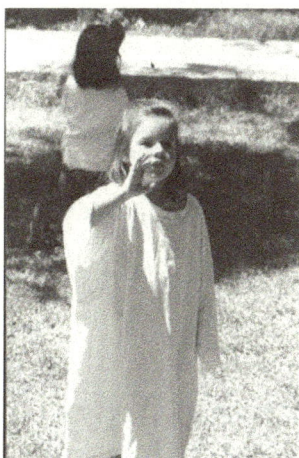

riding her tricycle,

or dressed up for

school.

A father will always

find it irresistibly funny to

terrorize and test his daughter's

prospective boyfriends.

A father will always

wonder what and how his daughter is doing

when she is not with him.

A father will always

throw her daughter high enough,

carry her on his back, and

make his shoulders

her throne of heavens.

A Father Is There . . .

. . .to show off his knowledge with his daughter

by responding to her persistent questioning,

from when she was sleepless as a little girl

until the day she asks for guidance.

. . .

. . .to teach his little girl, a future woman,

why she deserves to be treated well by men.

. . .

. . .to give his daughter confidence by showing

her that he believes in her strength

when she does not.

A father is there

to be present at his daughter's wedding

to the man she expects to be

similar to her father

and

to remain discreetly near,

as well as helpful, during those

unavoidable times of trial in her marriage.

A father is there

to show his daughter how to put aside for the

rainy days, how to spend sensibly, and how to

give to others, wholeheartedly and nobly.

. . .

To teach her that economy is a beautiful oak,

whereas misery is a nasty wormwood.

. . .

To restrain her from buying things

she doesn't need, with money she shouldn't

spare, to impress people she doesn't even like.

A father is there

to explain everything to his daughter

in relation to boys giving emphasis to the fact

that men will always hide a boy inside them

but this doesn't mean they always

remain less mature

than women.

And that's why her father

was always able to play like a child with her,

whereas her mother couldn't.

A father is there

so his daughter can understand

with dignity why and how she lost a battle

otherwise, she'll never learn how to win her wars.

A father is there

to show his daughter

that the sooner she realizes

that life is not going to be easy,

the better she'll be prepared to deal with

hardships and become a stronger person.

A father is there

to demonstrate for his daughter that character

is built from the bricks that life

will unexpectedly

throw at her;

even though it's not always possible to shield

and protect her, he will always

be there to help her

heal.

A father is there

to explain to his daughter

why her real friends will be those

who will talk to her face to face, and not about her

behind her back.

. . .

They are the ones who,

when she needs them, not only

they wont disappear, but they'll appear

uninvited and not quit even

if she discourages them.

A father is there

to convince his daughter that if her

relationships with her friends don't make her

a better person, then she is spending

her time with the wrong people.

A father is there

ready to become a happy, supportive,

and selfless grandfather

to his daughter's children.

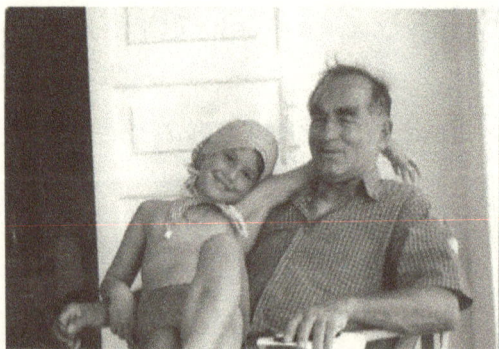

A father is there

to pass on to his daughter

some of his biggest secrets

in life:

that he only attained true happiness

when he managed to love and

not just to be loved,

and

that he achieved ultimate power

when he managed to conquer patience.

A Father Should . . .

. . . never forget that he represents the measure

by which his daughter will evaluate

every other man in her life,

and

that his way of life implies on a daily basis

what kind of a man his daughter should choose

for the father of her children.

A father should

in case of a divorce,

support her daughter's

relationship with her mother at all times,

irrespective of whether her mother doesn't do

the same.

A father should

show his daughter

that the path of sacrifice

is beneficial and serves its purpose only

when she decides to follow it with joyfulness,

and without seeking acknowledgment from

anyone else

but God.

A father should

instill in his daughter the perceptive that

offering help to others is mostly beneficial

for the person who offers.

A father should

be in the position to know when it's not "OK"

if his daughter says that everything is.

A father should

.

make sure his daughter knows that,

as a woman, she always and under all

circumstances will have an equal value

to any man;

she must never let anyone

tie her value to her appearance

(no matter what the latter is).

A father should

occasionally remind his grown-up daughter

that she is unlikely

to meet the loving, handsome, and

gentle man of her dreams

in a bar.

A father should

be the one to prove to

his daughter that the future

does not depend on men but on women,

by reminding her that even God Himself

was dependent on a woman to give, voluntarily

birth to His Son in order to save the world, and

that since then, His Son's Mother has

undertaken the role of intervening to her Son

for the salvation of all of us.

A father should

refrain during his daughter's teens

from spontaneously and loudly calling her

nicknames in front of her friends.

. . .

But he'll find that to be his most persuasive

threat— because he might do exactly that

at the first chance he gets.

A father should

never neglect to demonstrate

to his daughter that she must always respect

the differences in others, without feeling obliged

to accept them.

A father should

not let his daughter repeat upon her own

children the mistakes his mother

may have made on him

but, also, strongly

remind her that there's

a lot to imitate from her

grandmother's virtues.

A father should

find ways to transfer discipline and manners

to his daughter

even better and more

sensibly than his parents did.

A father should

try to contribute to road safety by,

at least, trying to make his daughter

a good driver,

and most importantly

trying to teach her

how to park a car correctly!

A father should

also not neglect to make his daughter a good

co-driver by teaching her to be patient with her

husband when he has to drive through an

inescapable pothole while she is putting

makeup on.

A father should

convince his daughter that the easy tears

help only during prayers,

and that ignorance

is not an excuse

that will always

work in her adult

life.

A father should

never miss out on the chance to devote

and dance with his daughter to

the Aerosmith song

"I don't wanna miss a thing."

A father should

never allow his daughter to be affected

by any small-minded person who tries to

tell her that her dreams are too big to realize,

but convince her that dreams, big or small,

deserve to come true, at the right time and in

the correct manner, and that only when

dreams turn into obsessions

should they be abandoned.

A father should

teach his daughter

the significance

of always being a lady,

because only then will she be

able to recognize a gentleman . . .

. . . who instead of fawning

is benign, who instead of treating

a woman as property shows her respect,

and who wants to invest his life in a woman

and not just spend money to show off.

A father should

encourage

his daughter to follow her heart. . .

. . .only if

she brings her brains along.

A father should

train his daughter to always find and pose

the right questions that will lead her to

the correct answers.

And,

never try to convince her

what to think and who to love,

but rather how to think and how to love.

A father should

help his daughter to develop and use her

emotional intelligence,

twice as much as her I. Q.

It is mainly through

empathy

that she will successfully

manage and guide the people around her

during life's inevitable

critical situations.

A father should

let his daughter know that

she must keep distance but no grudge

from the envious people

and that

too much kindness

will actually harm her

unremorseful 'friends'.

A father should

instill in his daughter faith in her capabilities,

but never more faith than she should have

in God and His powers . . .

. . . and remind her that life becomes

safer and securer when we increase our trust

in God and not just in

life, house, or car

insurances.

A Father Needs a Daughter . . .

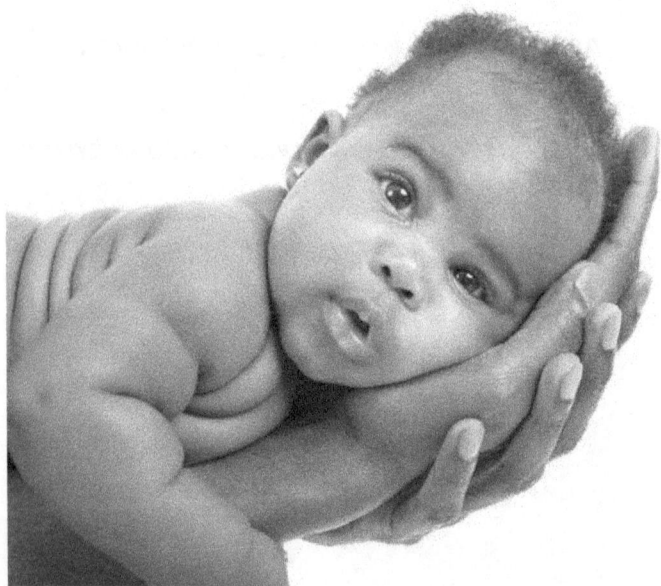

. . . to realize from the beginning that some

of the most precious things in his life

will be the experiences and the moments

he'll be able to share with her.

Like when his daughter was born and she was so

small that he could hold her in the palm of his hand,

when she ran into his arms

even though they were empty of gifts or treats,

when he was teaching her how to swim and trained

her for the deep waters of reality,

to when he was carrying her on his shoulders

and prepared her to always try to see

beyond the crowd. . .

A father needs a daughter

to remind him of the things

he will be forgetting

as he grows old.

A father needs a daughter

to ensure that he will never cease

to be needed, to be her haven

in the difficult times of her life

and to be able to follow

without restraint his tendency

to guide and share his wisdom—

anytime, anyplace!

A father needs a daughter

to pass on to her some

of the most crucial experiences of

his life that helped him built his own legacy.

Wasn't, one of them, the fact that he often met

and associated with people so poor, who's

only appreciated values were just

material goods and money,

that taught him the real

meaning poverty?

. . .

The real meaning of wealth

is a person's value

when he doesn't have any

or has lost all his money...

A father needs a daughter

so he can have the most serious

incentive to keep his promises,

to have a reason to avoid vice

and stay inside the path of virtue, and

to muster strength from her undoubted

trust, so when everything is deadlocked,

quitting is not an option for him.

A father needs a daughter

to learn when

he should be firm and

when he should compromise.

A father needs a daughter

so he can include in his life's arsenal

a balsam made from his daughter's

smiles and drawings,

so whenever he's wounded from sadness or

disappointment, he can take

a dose for courage.

A father needs a daughter

to be motivated and maintain his dignity

under all circumstances,

especially when he is

provoked.

A father needs a daughter

to have someone who won't undermine him,

will admire him, and will need him

especially when everyone else

abandons him.

A father needs a daughter

to have an extra reason

to turn back when

he heads in

the wrong

direction.

A father needs a daughter

because . . .

to a father growing old

nothing is dearer than a daughter!

(attributed to Euripides)

Please inscribe below your personal piece of legacy

and dedicate it to your father or daughter.